I HOPE MY VOICE

Alicia
Cook

DOESN'T SKIP

I Hope My Voice Doesn't Skip

Poems by Alicia Cook

*Written between August 2016
and January 2018*

Andrews McMeel
PUBLISHING®

This book grew
from many different soils,
with pages sprouting in

New Jersey
New York
Pennsylvania
Connecticut
South Carolina
California
Colorado
Hawaii
Mexico
Italy
Spain
France

Trigger Warning (TW):

Mental illness, death, drug use, violence, miscarriage

&

The poem "Ten Little Girls" includes the topics
of sexual assault, suicide, eating disorders,
body shaming, kidnapping, weapons,
death/murder, and drug use.

I think you should be nervous about
what I will accomplish once I heal.

The mountains I'll move.
The miles I'll cover.
The skin I'll get under.

—Stuff I've Been Feeling Lately

We are all recovering from something.
This is for all of us.

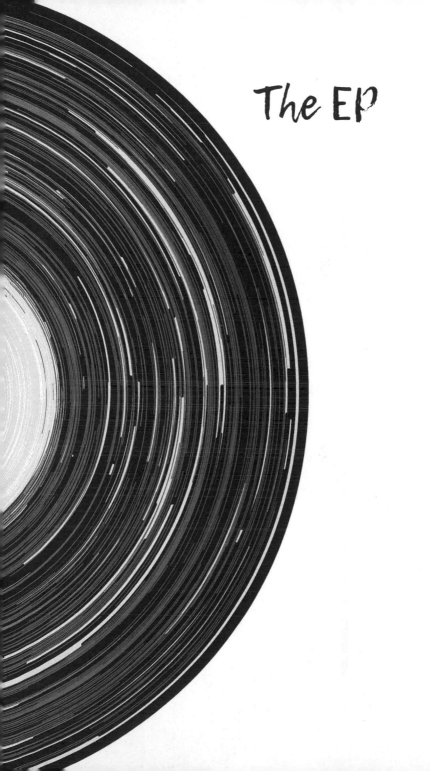

The EP

EP Track List

Lampyridae & Our Bioluminescence

The short years when we were children,
we would chase fireflies around the yard.
We would capture one and
peel the sticky light from its skin.
We would wear it on our fingers
like glowing diamonds; trophies.

How cruel I was to steal the light from this creature.
How naive I was to believe no one would ever
try to steal my light away.

How resilient I am to keep shining anyway.

The Denouement

I am
 sick and tired
 of swallowing the blood
 from biting my own tongue
 just so you do not have to
 swallow your pride.

But I am not like you;
 I am not a destroyer.
 I toy with the truths
 I keep trapped behind my lips.
 I mix them with my saliva until
 they are as smooth as river stones.

All I need to do
 is skip them across
 the sound barrier and
 you'd be exposed.

But I am not like you;
 I am not a killer.

Collateral Beauty

Tragedy leaks into the buckets of our bodies.
We don't realize we're cracked until
we've flooded and the pressure releases,
pouring out in tears from our eyes and
screams from our throats and
anger from our clenched fists and
prayers from our bended knees.

It is those same unassuming cracks
where grace enters to replenish us through
the light from our eyes and
the songs from our voices and
the humanity from our outstretched arms and
the new chapters from our forward-marching feet.

Hypnic Jerk

I find my voice is tired.
My vocal cords strained
from screaming over
my own self-doubt.
I find my voice is tired.

I find my heart is tired.
Each tick takes effort,
forced and erratic,
much like my smile.
I find my heart is tired.

I find my mind is tired.
Thoughts arrive slowly,
steering through the fog
of my murky brain.
I find my mind is tired.

I find my eyes are tired.
Each blink is heavy,
yearning to just sleep
some time away.
I find my eyes are tired.

I trust the process. I let them all rest.

Some Piranhas Are Vegetarians

I switch the song on the radio
because it reminds me of you and
I don't feel like visiting you today.
My mind understands the feelings
evoked by the music are illusions,
but try telling that to my soul.

You were not my person.
You were my lesson.

You were . . .
You were . . .

You were the piranha, circling.
I discovered too late that you
made a habit of attacking people
with hearts much larger than yours.

The '90s Seem So Long Ago

The smell of peeled oranges
makes me think of Thanksgiving.
The crisp crunch of raw celery
and the aroma of steam
rising from radiators reminds me
of my father on Christmas.

My childhood.
I used to breathe here.
Impatiently.

Now I look back,
fondly,
missing the sounds of a
crowded home with love
and arguments
and dogs yapping.

I remember it all,
eyes closed tight,
angry with myself that

I was ever impatient.

Fits

I outgrew you.
It saddened me greatly.
Like outgrowing
a favorite sweater
I wished still fit
because the fibers
felt so familiar and soft
against my skin.

But your mistakes
became your patterns
and your patterns
never looked good on me.

I Am Marked

They all can see
that I carry
what no one will address.

The guilt, the shame,
I've had enough,
I want to catch my breath.

The elephant
here in this room
is sitting on my chest.

And unbeknownst
to everyone,
he's crushing me to death.

Hemlock Falls & Fairy Houses

Everything is greener at the top of New Jersey,
including your eyes.

The waterfall is falling how I was;
fast, without remorse, naturally.

Once you sit down by the falls, I do the same,
putting a safe distance between me and you and
your hands and the spray of the water.

You notice the distance between us and
bait me to close   the   gap.

I stay put, blaming the puddle that formed between
us from the early morning rain.

I'm not afraid of a little water, you say and move closer.
Me either, I say, blowing my cover.

Saturday-Morning Cartoons

There's always a bad guy,
a three-year-old tells me
between playing with my thumb,
referring to a children's show.

He doesn't know much of anything yet,
but he knows this to be certain:

There's always a bad guy.

Riviera Maya

My lips have touched
so many salt-rimmed glasses today,
they have started to prune.

I am reminded of bath-soaked fingers and toes.

I live 1.2 miles from the hospital where I was born,
and flew to Mexico to watch two children of divorce
vow never to end up like their parents.

A testament to remembering where you came from,
but understanding you do not have to stay there.

Wandering, Wondering

We are walking
across the uncut grass.

I, barefoot,
you, in shoes.

This is how we differ.

*Do you ever wonder how many
four-leaf clovers we are crushing?* I ask.

Probably not a lot, you say.

This is where we differ.

Rome & My Ruins

After I am gone,
my words will be excavated.

Dug up,
dusted off,
preserved.

My cross-outs that never became thoughts,
my thoughts that never became words.

Perhaps a lingering eyelash or
finger smudge will reveal itself.

And my words will be shared,
and I will speak again.

Disquietude

I let the rain collect
on the windshield because
the noise from the wipers hurts my ears.

I let you remain in
the passenger seat for
another day because the sound
of goodbye hurts my heart.

There's the Rub

You were weak.

You were weak, and you gave up.
You were weak and took the coward's way out.
You were weak, and you left without a word.

It doesn't take much strength
to slam the door
of an empty room.

I was strong, and I locked it behind you.
I was strong, and I cried.
I was strong, and I moved on.

I was strong.

Amalfi Coast

I wash the Mediterranean Sea from my hair,
it slicks down my face,
drips from my nose to my lips.

I find I'm smiling.

Some days really are
good enough to taste.

I brush the breeze from my hair,
pick the sand from my fingernails,
and watch as the last seven hours
swirl down the drain.

Some days really do
leave their mark.

If Only Romeo Were Running Late
to Her Funeral

My desire for you has become palpable.
I dream we kiss, and I wake up aroused.

Wrong timing makes for
star-crossed lovers
and lethal thoughts.

The tension has manifested itself in other ways.
Today, in the tearing of napkins and straw wrappers.

What will happen when the paper runs out?
When *I want you* turns into *I need you.*
When *I shouldn't* turns into *I can't help myself.*

Pressed Dandelions

I keep weeds in a vase
in my living room.
I feed them water.
I bathe them in sunlight.

A child picked them for me,
believing they were flowers.

Who am I to tell him
not all pretty things
are worthy of saving,
just as not all things
worth saving are pretty.

Dive

I have been daydreaming, treacherously.
You and I, we slow dance in this dream.
I do not dance; but with you,
I imagine it would be nice.

Pressed together.
Heartbeat to heartbeat.
Palms and lifelines kissing.

Swaying to words we cannot say
but feel nonetheless.

Absent

We aren't here forever.
Sometimes, the conclusion
will come suddenly
and arrive much too close
to the beginning.

We will feel robbed.
We will be mad at time.

Yet, no matter how fleeting,
I pray we can say,

It wasn't a long while,
but it was worthwhile.
It wasn't a long life,
but it was a wonderful life.

"I Am Sorry for Your Loss"

When someone we love dies,
we say we *lost* them.
Perhaps this is our mind's way
of convincing our hearts
we will one day find them again.

Mellifluous Monotony

The ice machine erupts,
falling rocks.

I smile at the sound of this routine from bed.

Every night
you bring me a glass of water.

Even though you know, I never take a sip.
Even though you know, the condensation rings
will be a bitch to wipe up come morning.

Obsequious

I will stay

but

I will not keep you	happy
I will not keep you	faithful
I will not keep you	here
I will not keep you	long.

You will tell me
it is because I cannot be kept   happy
faithful
here
long.

I will not keep you; but I will stay.

Broken Hearts & Brokenhearted People

The first time my heart was broken,
I buried my mirror image with whom I shared a last
name and affinity for sushi and hot sauce.

She was broken, and brokenhearted people break people.

The second time my heart was broken
was when I broke someone else's.

I was broken, and brokenhearted people break people.

Traffic, Signs

I only ever noticed the wildflowers
growing along Interstate 84
when I was in the passenger seat of your car.

Bright orange and purple magic,
granting wishes in the forced wind
of the speeding cars.

So vibrant.
So hard to believe I never once
noticed them before.

I like to think you slowed my world down.
I like to think you opened my eyes.

Basilicata

It scares me,
how young I will still be at my oldest.

The weight of my mortality could kill me
as I sit in a 3,000-year-old city.

I curse the precarious nature of my existence.
I haven't yet bathed in enough salt water,
smelled enough of my mother's cooking.
I haven't woken up enough times
with morning on my breath.
I haven't gotten enough bee stings or paper cuts.

I will never be ready to leave.

Check & Mate

I see you seeing me.
Not sure why you continue to stare.
I haven't glanced in your general direction
in quite some time.

You keep competing, but
that doesn't mean you are winning.

You see,
I stopped playing the game
once I realized I was being played, and
that sure as hell doesn't feel like losing.

Day at Sea

I sit curled up in an oversized, comfortable chair,
reading a book that only made it to
the *New York Times* Best Sellers' list
because it was written by a dead girl.

The caramel wicker is smooth to the touch.
The sun shines on the deck;
to my right, the endless Atlantic,
to my left, my beating heart.

I wonder how I got here.
I wonder when I became lucky enough
to ask myself this question.

A Meteorological Phenomenon

I saw a rainbow today.

I experienced a lot more,
like a flat tire and a French kiss,
but the rainbow is what I wish to remember.

Though I know it's merely a reflection
and dispersion of light, I imagine
what it would feel like to touch its bends.

I close my eyes, reach,
and dip my hands into the colors like wet paint.

And for one brief moment,
I am part of the iridescence.

Hard of Hearing

Tell me I will get over it.
Tell me I feel this way because I am young.
Tell me I will laugh about it when I am older.
Tell me I am overreacting.
Tell me I deserve better.
Tell me I am inexperienced and
that's why I am distraught.
Tell me I am being dramatic.
Tell me my eyes will clear.
Tell me I will smile again.

Tell me how to heal—*I didn't hear you the first time.*

The Send-Off & Homecoming

There's a fleeting romance found
in the one-way ticket,
but there's undeniable comfort
in the round-trip.

Though I explore—
collecting passport stamps,
hotel points and keycards,
tiny shampoo bottles,
and airline miles,
I cannot imagine never
looking back,
never returning.
I cannot fathom ever
losing sight of the familiar horizon of home.

Glimmers

Even in the midst of my darkest days,
there were minutes—moments—
flickers of light.

A smile through fear.
A pleasant dream stitched between
the threads of a perpetual nightmare.
A sunny day that transiently warmed
a heart that had been soaked by torrential rain.
A restorative kiss that healed
ten scraped knuckles and a battered mind.

These small offerings of hope
were all I needed to believe again
long enough to make it to the other side.

The LP

LP Track List

Sailing On

I sing *Anchors, aweigh!*
as I make my way
away
from my old ways.

Though I fear less
and less each day,
I am still not quite fearless.

Seemingly
bursting at the seams,

but this momentary might
might not
make me mighty.

To err is human, yes,
but I need fresh air
to air my grievances.

Like how your apologies
need apologies.

Like how walking away
was my biggest feat
since my feet stepped up
and took their first steps.

Do not remain unfazed.
No, it is not *just a phase.*

Speaking out
doesn't make me outspoken,
it makes me heard
over the herd.

The Stains Left Behind

You lose someone, and their ghost splatters
everywhere. Black as squid ink in the fibers of your
clothes. In the ringlets of your unwashed hair. In the
last glass from which they drank. In the passenger
seat of your car. The impression of their spoon in the
sugar bowl matches your hollowness.

Then life continues. The splatter fades. You wash
your clothes and your hair. You clean the dirty dishes
and refill the sugar bowl. Maybe you buy a new car or
move into a place whose entryway they have never
danced through.

The sun still rises every day, the world still spins. You
brush your teeth and replace the empty toilet paper
roll. You walk your dogs. You set morning alarms
and hear new music.

Life pushes you along,
routine keeps you breathing.

Everything that they've touched with their hands,
heart, or eyes is given away or pushed to the back of
your mind and closet, or moved into the attic. Not on
purpose. Not because you want to forget they existed
here with you, but because you kept existing and you
accept that though you cannot recall what their voice
sounded like, you will never forget how they made
you feel.

Leaf-Strewn Sidewalks

The leaves still hold a glow, swirling and fluttering from the trees in Bryant Park. I try to remember, recall if the leaves are avoiding the inevitable longer than this time last year.

Perhaps the branches are the ones
that are refusing to let go this year.

I know what it is like to clutch on to something for as long as I can possibly stand, even when what I wanted to keep was dead. I am constantly caught between being afraid I will always remember and being afraid I'll forget one day. Not a unique thought or feeling, I am sure.

The sound of the wind funneling through these buildings reminds me of the ocean crashing, and for a moment, my two worlds collide; but I am in this world now far more than the other.

Skylines and high-rises and busy streets have replaced much of what I had known where I once found my feet. I wish when people asked me what I wanted to be when I grew up, I was smart enough to respond: *What's the rush?*

Dear God

Lucid moments with her are
fewer and far between.
She is, but I'm not,
forgetting who she used to be.

God tell me what to do
when you lose a person who
is still standing in front of you.

Dear God,
please don't take her
away from me;
there is still so much in life
she has yet to see.
Like true love,
nephews and nieces—
and things with time,
like old-age creases.

Dear God, please,
allow her just one more turn
to take back her life and learn
that she is here for a reason—
that this cold weather
is nothing but a passing season.

Show her clearer days
can be found ahead;
but none of this is possible,
if she is first found dead.

God, you have shown me
the Devil lives in this powder;
and if you can't hear my plea,
I promise to pray louder.

Motor Skills

I am losing track of myself again.
I can feel it in my restlessness.
In the picking of my cuticles.
In the cracking of my knuckles.
In the playing with my hair.
In the wandering of my eye.
In my fatigue.

*"Something wicked
this way comes."*[1]

I've been drinking the same iced coffee all day.
The dilution is off-putting but not deterring.

I release my hands from the steering wheel
as I drive down the Garden State Parkway.
They ache terribly. I must have been gripping
the wheel much tighter than I realized.

I make fists and then release,
welcoming the feeling
returning to my fingers.

I pay little attention to the mile markers
as I make my way down the same highway
I've traveled countless times before.

Muscle memory will get me there.
It always has.

---

[1]From Act 4, Scene 1 of *Macbeth* by William Shakespeare

This Isn't About the Number Six

6 weeks before you died, we sat together.
You were sad, and I was mad,
but we managed to laugh and joke
about our crazy mothers.

We ate sandwiches together.
We hugged and we shared our last words.
Of course, we didn't know then
they would be our last.

6 seconds before I knew you were dead,
I wasn't thinking about you.
I was thinking about the test
I had just sat down to take.
It was on Shakespeare's Sonnets.

Then my
phone rang.

6 seconds after I knew you were dead,
you were all I could think of;
I flipped through my memory,
tried to recall our last words.
I couldn't remember, and I left class in tears.

6 minutes after I knew you were dead,
my phone rang again.
It was my mother,
frustrated with my father
for telling me about you
before I got home.

I was already driving home.
My parents were nervous
I wouldn't be able
to concentrate on the road,

but I made it home fine.

6 hours after I knew you were dead,
I went on social media.
I wrote, *I will miss eating french fries with you.*
I knew you would know what I meant.

66 hours after you died, I saw you for the last time.
Your father screamed my name. *I still hear it.*
The lipstick you were wearing did not look right.
My mother whispered to someone to change it,

and they did.

I read a prayer at your funeral.
I can't remember the name.

Your father eulogized you;
his love for you kept his knees from buckling.

Your mother took a nap.
She woke up crying so loud
we heard her from the first floor.

I saw my father cry for the first time
as he hugged your father,
who bought a suit he has not worn since.
I watched my father kiss your casket.

6 days after you died, my mother turned 50.
She didn't want to celebrate
her birthday that year,

      so we didn't.

6 weeks after you died, I ate an entire loaf of bread.
I was with your mother and grandmother.
Your grandmother died shortly after,
I believe from a broken heart.

6 months after you died, you turned 20.
I promised myself we would celebrate
your 21st the following year.

      We did.

I found my journal;
you know the one.
I turned to the last page
and found I had recorded our last words.

      I'll see you later, Cuz.

6 Christmases after you died,
your parents still hadn't put up a tree.
I went to church,
wanting to light a candle in your name.
Two times the candle wouldn't light.
Very funny! I exclaimed to the ceiling. *To you.*
On the third attempt, the candle sparked.

      I smiled.

6 years after you died, I got married
to someone you would have met if
you had survived 6 months longer.
You appeared in the slideshow, and your father
looked at me and mouthed, *Thank you.*
I still don't know why he was thanking me;
I wanted to see your face, too.

600 weeks after you died,
I am having dinner with your sister.
We discuss if losing you has made us stronger.

I don't want to be stronger, she tells me.
I just want my sister back.

For You

Everyone thought I was the strong one,
but I wasn't strong.

I broke out in hives. I slept two hours a night, only to
wake up startled and out of breath, with my heart
beating so hard against my ribs that it was painful.
I cried in the shower, I vomited, I fainted.
I either ate nothing or binged.

No, I wasn't strong.
I was an emotional mess who just kept it together,
who remembered to breathe and smile
in front of my parents.

The person who stayed when no light at the end of
the tunnel was in sight, who waited while
I cried, itched, slept all day, or tossed and turned,
made myself sick, didn't shower for days, or used up
all the hot water, is the strong one in this story.

I've learned you will always have to save yourself,
but it is easier to keep fighting with someone in your
corner.

2,000 Forecasts

Reading by candlelight,
it was cold that October night.
Drunk off six-dollar wine,
the hurricane raging outside.

That night we slept wrapped in quilts,
talking about our neighborhood
and what had to be rebuilt.

I couldn't see through the blackness
that night on your mattress,
but I felt your telltale heart,
it promised us a fresh start.

2,000 forecasts have passed
since you last smiled and asked
me what we'd name our children.

The memory plays the first crisp day
and my heart always gives way,
relives us when the leaves descend.

We survived the storm but not the fall.
We survived the storm but not the fall.

After two nights of freezing,
kissing noses running, sneezing;
after a roller-coaster drowning,
80-mile-per-hour winds howling,

the house buzzed again with power.
You celebrated in your boxers
and I joined you in the shower.

Empty glasses left in the sink,
your ice eyes and that wink.
The heat was rising, you held me near;
you sang The Turtles in my ear.

2,000 forecasts have passed
since you last smiled and asked
me what we'd name our children.

The memory plays the first crisp day
and my heart always gives way,
relives us when the leaves descend.

We survived the storm but not the fall.
We survived the storm but not the fall.

I wore your shirt to bed those days.
I still have it, the sleeves have frayed.
I surely would have froze to death
if I didn't know you or share your breath

for that one brief, long moment.

But we survived the storm,
not the fall.

We were the storm
and we're better off.

Hiraeth

Yesterday I cooked bacon because the smell reminds me of my father and Saturday mornings in that old house on Valley Street across from the railroad tracks. Back when we had one television that took twenty minutes to turn on. Back when I shared a bedroom with both of my siblings. Back when that Billy Joel cassette melted in the tape deck of my mother's light-blue Thunderbird.

Back when we searched for goldfish in the stone pond my father unearthed in the backyard on my little brother's birthday. Back when the aroma of citronella torches was synonymous with summer. Back when our grandfather was still alive and brought us doughnuts in a white box tied with a candy cane–striped ribbon. Back when my mother used to sing "Que Sera, Sera" to my sister every evening before our good-night prayer.

That old two-family house, with white siding, where we used to play on the front porch and pluck thorns from my parents' rosebushes. Where the Christmas tree fell down one year in the middle of the night. Where we used to yank up oniongrass just to smell it, and where we touched our tongues to honeysuckle flowers.

As the bacon tap-danced in the skillet, I imagined mail was being delivered to the house I still occasionally drive past. Though I may never walk up those cracked stone steps again, or hear the swing of that particular kitchen door, there's a deep security felt when a simple scent floods me with memories that only a handful of people I love could recognize.

Nightmares & Daydreams

Featuring J.R. Rogue (www.jrrogue.com)

I have nightmares;
and I'm not talking about
the kind that grab you with
their ebony grip while
the rest of the street slumbers.

I have daydreams;
and I'm not talking about
the kind that seduce my
smile out of hiding
and color me senseless.

I have scars;
and I'm not talking about
the two on my stomach
from when I was on dialysis
or the one on my finger from when
I was doing cartwheels and
landed on a broken glass bottle.

I have imperfections;
and I'm not talking about
the chip in my left tooth
or my crazy hair.

I have faith;
and I'm not talking about
the intangible kind.
I'm talking about the breathing soul asleep
on the pillow next to mine.

Four Minutes in May

12:07 p.m.

The wind chimes get swept up in the *not-quite-yet-summer* breeze along with the *not-quite-dry* shirts on the clothesline.

The sun breaks through the clouds, offering the promise of a wonderful day. I breathe in the first few hints of my second-favorite season.

12:09 p.m.

The telephone rings.

12:11 p.m.

I remain in the lounge chair, suddenly angry at the breeze for blowing life into clothes you will never wear again.

Hindsight & Pictures

Featuring Christopher Andrews

You and I, nothing but a mess.
Dressed
like the best
love story that ever was;
but we were
a fatal mixture,
just pretty
in hindsight and pictures.

You and I, a flawed design.
Lines
blurred between
the pleasure and so much pain.
So save me
all of your lectures,
we're only real
in hindsight and pictures.

You and I, in such distress.
Nonetheless,
we soaked in
the glory and the applause.
Gettin' off,
gettin' sicker, while that
grapevine whispered.
Oh, hindsight and pictures.

You and I, I left behind.
Unsatisfied,
with the monsters
we became, so I severed.
Cut the tether
to that fatal mixture
'cause we're only livin'
in hindsight and pictures.

Hindsight and pictures.
A fatal mixture.
Hindsight and pictures.
Save me the lecture.
Hindsight and pictures.
Grapevine whispers.
Hindsight and pictures.
A fatal mixture.
Hindsight and pictures.

Listen to "Hindsight & Pictures":
www.thealiciacook.com/chrisandrews

Gloves on Radiators

It is one of those days when it is so cold everything takes on a frosty-blue hue. I take a dangerously deep breath, and my throat stings. Water would soothe it, but it is all frozen. Kids pretend they are smoking cigarettes each time they exhale, and noses, drainpipes, and windowsills collectively weep all around. Their sadness is loud.

Plop. Plop. Plop.

The sound reminds me of my mother
dropping ice cubes into our soups.

Does it hurt to melt?

I imagine they cry because they miss the warmth of the sun and freckled noses and blooming pots on ledges. It is one of those days where I make pancakes and poached eggs because that's what we've always done when winter makes itself known.

The first thing I ever told the first person I fell in love with was that I hated snow. One lifetime later and I still stand by that statement even though I no longer stand by that man.

I count forward on my calendar, to the first day of spring.

One, two, three . . .

Where my pointer finger lands is where I find relief.

Detergent & Denial

I sit on my laundry room floor just watching the dryer
spin my clothes around and around.

Da thump.
Da thump.
Da thump.

If I get up
and go upstairs,
I need to say it aloud.
Saying it aloud will make it real.
I'm not ready to make it real yet.
If I stay here instead,
only the spider webbing in the corner
and I will know what we know.

I remain on my laundry room floor, phone in hand,
heart beating in my chest.

Da thump.
Da thump.
Da thump.

Machines and humans share similar sounds.
They break the same, too.

Aunt Em

Featuring Renee Mazza

Oh, Dorothy,

please open your eyes.
Silence cuts like knives.
You've been gone for days.
Our world has gone gray
without your smile here.

Oh, Dorothy,

Dear, are you awake
in some far-off place?
Your eyelids shudder,
can't help but wonder
if your dreams bring fear.

I hope your brain never scatters,
your heart never shatters,
and the courage you gather
brings you back to me.

May the wicked witches never hurt you.
May you meet friends who support you.
May a bright-yellow road return you
back to me.

Oh, Dorothy,

my eyes haven't slept,
but oh how they've wept.

I Hope My Voice Doesn't Skip

The hourglass sand
holds the upper hand
as we sit beside your bed.

Oh, Dorothy,

the tornado destroyed,
created this void.
You're missing it all;
like the simple songs
from birds overhead.

I hope your bright brain never aches,
your heavy heart never breaks,
and your courage shapes
your path back to me.

May the air from a hot balloon ride you.
May three clicks of your heels glide you.
May the glow from a rainbow guide you
back to me.

Oh, Dorothy,

return from where you roam.
Trust me when I tell you:
There's no place like home.

Listen to "Aunt Em": www.thealiciacook.com/reneemazza

Odylic Force

You tell me as long as I don't smile at you,
you can stay composed, and my face flushes.

You warm me when you sneak up behind me,
nudging my lower back, and I imagine what your
weight would feel like on top of my body.

I tell you I enjoy being around you and ask how your
day is going, but what I really want to know is

Do you ever dream of me?

Because I dream of you.
In the most vivid of colors.
In the most dangerous of ways.

I tell you that I like how your socks match your tie
and ask how your weekend was,
but what I really want to know is

What happens to your body when I walk into a room?

Because when we are in shared space,
so much fresh air enters my lungs,
they feel new.

The day starts over.
You reset me and have no idea.

I think your eyes sparkle
when they meet mine,
but it could just be a cruel trick of light.

Springtime in the Cemetery

I.

I am a child, holding my great-grandmother's hand
as we weave between the tombstones.

I free myself and begin walking very close to the
graves of long-gone strangers.

Do not walk directly on top of them, she warns
Do not disrespect the dead like that.

II.

Three years later, I am seated in that very same
cemetery, at my great-grandmother's funeral; a dog
barks in the distance.

My siblings play hide-and-seek behind
the stones and trees.

Do not disrespect the dead like that, I repeat to them,
not sure at the time what that means.

III.

Many years later, a toddler holds my hand
as we follow a funeral procession to the tent.

Where are we? he asks.

We are at a park, I lie, because a lie is easier than
explaining death.

But people don't cry in parks, he says back.

IV.

My parents learn the cemetery is developing new
land and decide now is the time to purchase
their plots.

They buy a few extra in case my husband and I
decide we want to rest there, too.

V.

My father returns with graveyard dirt under his nails.
He tells me it is not really Easter until you visit your
dead.

You're the Worst

I was carrying the weight of your abandonment
and it callused my hands,
broke my spirit,
froze my heart.

I let go,
out of necessity,
and learned you
were the worst thing
to ever happen to me.

I know this because
once the pain faded,
you faded.
Entirely. Gone. *Poof.*

If you were anything more than
just plain old hurt,
you would still live in my memory,
still find yourself nestled comfortably
in even the smallest nook of my heart.

You were pain,
and I don't hold on to pain anymore.

I let go.
I lived.

If you were the worst
to ever happen to me,
the best is yet to come.

Ten Little Girls (TW)

Modeled after the nursery rhyme "Ten Little Indians"

Ten little girls get bullied online;
one hangs herself,
so now, there's nine.

Nine little girls restrict food intake;
one destroys her kidneys,
so now, there's eight.

Eight little girls all turn 11;
an uncle touches one,
so now, there's seven.

Seven little girls touch food to their lips;
one develops bulimia,
so now, there's six.

Six little girls go for a drive;
one is texting and steering,
so now, there's five.

Five little girls sneak in a drawer;
a gun accidentally goes off,
so now, there's four.

Four little girls lose their virginities;
one gets pregnant,
so now, there's three.

I Hope My Voice Doesn't Skip

Three little girls take a pill that's blue;
one quickly overdoses,
so now, there's two.

Two little girls just want to have fun;
one gets kidnapped,
so now, there's one.

One little girl remains out of 10;
there's got to be one success story
every now and then.

Transitions

I smell rain.

The world outside is too loud today.
Car horns and leaves scratching on the pavement
like city tumbleweeds wake up my anxiety.
People yell in a language I can't understand,
but by the tone, I can tell they're angry.
Everyone seems so angry lately.

The early November air plays perfectly
with my hair and blows life into my lungs
but somehow manages to miss my heart.

Clouds roll in and, in the distance,
the rumble of thunder erupts and
a car alarm goes off in response.

More noise.

I sacrifice the breeze and close the windows
on all four of my heart's hammering chambers.

This world sure is beautiful
without all the noise we make.

The falling rain splits the afternoon open,
allowing room for self-reflection
in the middle of this loud day.

I Hope My Voice Doesn't Skip

Another autumn leaf floats
to the ground somewhere,
I can feel it.

Five minutes of quiet is all I need to regroup.
I gather my breaths and
roll down my windows once again.

I take a deep lungful of
this beautiful, rarefied air,
full of life and sound and emotion,
that even the grateful
take for granted
from time to time.

I smell resurgence.

It's About Power

You were *almost always* gone.

One arm in the sleeve of your jacket.
One foot out the door.
The selfish fluidity was paralyzing.

Were you fifteen minutes late or
already fifteen miles closer to your next life?

It took a long time to realize I gave you that power.

The power to leave.
The power to come back.
The power to be in two places at once.

Sometimes prying your power back from the hands of someone accustomed to abusing your love means breaking your heart one last time. Hurting to heal will be painful at first, but nowhere near the agony of hurting to stay.

The Process of Apoptosis

There is no comfort in change. It is foreign and prickly; fiberglass on your arms, ice on your back molars, that hard bite of Jell-O. Change stretches our bones and minds to uncomfortable lengths without warning and then expects us to grow into it quickly.

There is no peace in losing someone. It is disruptive. It is heartbreaking and disharmonious; nails on a chalkboard, a fork scraping on a plate.

There is no beauty in pain. We imagine there to be, though. The beauty born from pain is man-made, created by the writers and the dreamers who romanticize recollections. Pain is ugly. No one should long for pain. No one should chase after pain. When pain does find you, you won't see any beauty—just blackness. Don't you ever forget it.

The comfort and peace and beauty are found in the reclaiming of your life in spite of it all.

Too

Featuring Caitlin Mahoney

It's the feeling we've met before,
somewhere in our other lives,
and we've been brought back to this one
through space and time, and by design.
None of this feels ordinary.
You are my very first déjà vu.
Do you feel it, too?

Tell me you feel it, too.
That the hazel flecks in your eyes
recognize my royal blue.
Tell me you feel it, too.

I've tasted your tongue, memorized
the songs our sighs sing as we rest.
I swear my hair already knows
the bliss of sleeping on your chest.
We are lightning and striking twice.
You are my familiar brand-new.
Do you feel it, too?

Tell me you feel it, too.
That we've both been uninspired,
tired, waitin' on a breakthrough.
Tell me you feel it, too.

My palms miss your hands and long to
hold them in this reality.
The years are long, and I'm not sure
how I survived the first thirty.

My eyelids have kissed your lips.
You're Christmas on Park Avenue.
Do you feel it, too?

Tell me you feel it, too.
That you spent years digging up lies
to unearth this one epic truth.
Tell me you feel it, too.
That you spent your whole life running
and standing still is overdue.
Tell me you feel it, too.

Listen to "Too":
www.thealiciacook.com/caitlinmahoney

Contrails

Today the sky is so pretty, I imagine Heaven is hanging a little lower to keep a closer eye on us for the day. A fellow golden hour admirer pulls out her phone and snaps a few images, whispering to herself, *It's like Heaven on Earth.*

The phrase stuck with me the rest of the day. *Heaven on Earth.* I hadn't heard it in a while. I hadn't heard it since I lost you, actually. I imagined what it would be like if Heaven could really pay us a visit.

We'd be able to walk side by side with people we love who we lost, and never forget the sound of their voice or their scent.

We would never know the pain that goes hand in hand with our impermanence here on the ground.

Simply put, it would be amazing.

"All We See or Seem Is but a . . ."[2] (TW)

To the observer,
my life has begun to orbit around
black-tie weddings, vacations, successes,
and bottomless brunches.

In reality,
my life revolves around
the marriages and divorces of my friends,
their pregnancies and miscarriages,
becoming parents and losing parents,
the overachieving of some and
the overdoses of others,
strands of our hair turning gray or
losing it all to chemo.

As I stand on this rooftop bar,
surrounded by café lights and muddled drinks,
I'll nurse this one glass of Chardonnay
and clutch these condensation-soaked napkins
I've been holding on to all night,
and I'll pay for a cab ride home
even though I could just drive myself.

Some days, it is simply easier to pretend
we are all as fortunate and as beautiful
as their general presuppositions.

---

[2] From the poem "A Dream Within a Dream" by Edgar Allan Poe

Am I Doing This Right?

A woman I know told me her wedding song came on while her husband was away for business and she cried in the shower. Another woman I know told me she gave up her career to move across the country with her fiancé so he could pursue his lifelong dream. Another told me they plan on having three kids and buying a house on a cul-de-sac. She used the term *forever home,* and for some reason, it made me feel sick. Another told me she preserved her wedding dress in a shadow box and just stares at it some lazy Sundays. A young girl I know told me she spends most of class time scribbling her and her beloved's initials in her notebook. I don't have the heart to tell her that her first love will also be her first heartbreak.

I know I love you, but I feel like I am doing it wrong.

I don't cry when you are away, and I would have to think long and hard before I gave up my goals in exchange for yours. Three kids are two too many. I bought the first wedding dress I tried on, and since we exchanged vows, it's been at the bottom of a hamper, slowly turning yellow. I never scribbled your name anywhere. I began a scrapbook of us years ago and abandoned the project the very same day.

I have never been below average in anything I pursued, but looking at the love stories of others, I feel as though I fall short of giving you all you deserve. I might not be capable.

Then, my mind calmed when, in the quiet of the home we created, I found myself picking up your purple sweatshirt and breathing in deep because I missed your scent.

I know I love you, and you know, too.

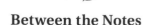

Between the Notes

Featuring Highland Kites

I visit our spot every once in a while.
Hear melodies of reconcile.
I sway between the notes and the Lilies of the Nile,
I remember when we danced in time,
but our music has ceased.

I trace our initials in the dock's creases.
A lifetime has passed since we
carved those masterpieces.

You and I,
You and I are unsolved dissonance.
Our chorus, our chords took on a bitterness.
Our love, our hate faded to indifference.
My body, it shakes, as I try to make sense of it.
I try to make sense of it.

Our hearts now beat at different tempos.
I'm giving up, giving in, letting go.
I don't wish back the time we borrowed.
I will remember when you were mine,
when the summer sun glows.

It's been a long ride, but I need you to know
despite what was lost in the fall,
we had something beautiful.

You and I,
You and I are unsolved dissonance.
Our chorus, our chords took on a bitterness.
Our love, our hate faded to indifference.
My body, it shakes, as I try to make sense of it.
I try to make sense of it.

I walk to our dock,
cold water on my feet
I know you've already
forgotten me.

I sit at our dock, the water lapping.
I don't think of you much at all these days
But I hope you are somewhere, happy.

Listen to "Between the Notes":
www.thealiciacook.com/highlandkites

The Beleaguered Ones

I am at war with choices I didn't make but have to live with nonetheless. I understand it's a counterstrike battle because the attacker was not aiming at me, but I've been hit. It's impossible to dodge stray bullets because you never see them coming, do you? The impact might not always be fatal, but the impact always hurts. *The gravel in my throat and eyes, it hurts.*

I've been grazed and hit precisely by life's blows because someone I love was targeted. Someone I love was the mark, but I am left wounded in the street. The collateral damage in all of this gets to die alongside the ones we love, but we die and our ghosts are left here to clean up messes and pick out coffins.

Our burial sites are shallow graves; dressed as twisted receiving lines where *I am sorry for your loss* is repeated in our faces every two seconds. I read once that it was rumored the Catholic Church was doing away with Purgatory, what some call Limbo, and I am starting to think that is because our lives become Purgatory when we lose someone we love.

More Than Mere Limerence

I didn't fall for you on purpose,
but it's never really on purpose I suppose.
It all happens slowly, doesn't it?

Between coffees and drinks and shared glances.
It sneaks up on you . . .

the
fall
ing.

They get under your skin. Your knees nudge and
your fingers linger as you pretend to argue over
who's going to pick up the check. You become more
curious so you ask more questions and suddenly you
find yourself waking up easier on days you know you
are going to see each other.

Then they begin to appear in your dreams, and you
start to wonder what they do for fun or how they look
naked. It is exciting and terrifying. You battle
between shaking them off or giving in, grabbing their
face, and kissing them just to see what their mouth
tastes like.

Saint Anthony

When I was a child, I wore my favorite gold bracelet every day. One day I looked down to find it was no longer there. My stomach dropped and I began to cry.

Where did you see it last? my mother asked.

The beach, maybe. I couldn't recall.

Pray to Saint Anthony, she suggested.

I must have repeated the prayer twenty times as my mother and I scoured the sand with flashlights.

Dear Saint Anthony / Please come down /
There is something lost / That needs to be found.
Dear Saint Anthony / Please come down /
There is something lost / That needs to be found.
Dear Saint Anthony / Please come down/
There is something lost / That needs to be found.

I tapped into my heart, into my faith, and truly prayed for Saint Anthony to return my bracelet. And the jewelry turned up and returned to its home upon my wrist.

As I've grown and begun to experience the loss of things more precious to me than that bangle,

like people,
like you,
I apply the same practice.

Dear Saint Anthony / Please come down /
There is something lost / That needs to be found.

I search my heart, and I find you there every time.

Original Christmas Song

My father still strings twinkling
white lights for me
across that timeworn tree
outside my old bedroom
I visit only occasionally.

A grown family of five
arrive home separately now.
No longer are there early
mornings spent in nightgowns.

The winter's been colder,
we're getting older,
I feel Christmas moving further
from what it used to be.

But Mom still decorates the tree,
while Bing and Danny Kaye sing,
and I am with my family.
This is what Christmas means to me.

"Have Yourself a Merry Little Christmas" plays.
Nostalgia, in waves,
as I remember days
as though it were yesterday
when all of our stockings hung in one place.

I'll never take the magic
for granted ever again.
I'll remember this wonderland
and what it all meant.

The winter's been colder,
we're getting older,
I feel Christmas moving further
from what it used to be.

But there's still record player static
and wrapping paper havoc,
taking trains down from the attic.
This is what Christmas means to me.

The smell of pine,
sparkling wine.
Italian tradition,
feast of the seven fishes.
Velvet dresses,
Mom cleaning up messes.
The smell of peppermint,
snowy footprints.
No school for a week,
kisses on cheeks.
Everyone's gleeful,
singing at the Cathedral.
Tree trimming,
Dad always filming.
Cousins playing games,
Grandpa misspelling my name.
Cold weather,
and a family, together.

This is what Christmas means to me.

Buried Alive

I have started over many times, but repetition does not make anything easier. The pain is in the details, in the shadows and crosshatching of our smiles and frowns.

I am not going to lie and tell you starting over was easy. It was so hard. Most will lie and tell you it was the easiest decision they ever made. I am not sure that they lie purposefully. I think once we start over, we forget how hard it was to shed our skin. Painful, even, to outgrow our own bones. Even when starting over is a choice and not a force of your hand, it still may be the hardest thing. We just forget how difficult it really was, because sometimes the hardest thing is also the best thing.

I will not lie and tell you that you will not cry, even when you make the best decision for yourself. I have mourned myself. I have grieved. Few hold an appreciation of life that only comes from being on the brink of death. That only comes from having to claw your way out of your own grave.

". . . But the North Ward Is the North Ward"[3]

I.

There were seven shootings in my city last night. The news didn't go national because only one of the seven shootings proved fatal. I happen to know in that very same city, that very same day, a child learned how to ride a bike. A family barbecued. A young woman blew out her thirtieth-birthday candles.

II.

My neighbor's home was broken into twice in one week. It is what it is. I put the security camera sign back up and measured my basement windows for wrought iron bars. I've since heard more laughter, ice cream truck music, and dogs barking than sirens.

III.

I pick up my friend from the airport. Once we get on McCarter Highway, the traffic slows because the Devils' game is just letting out. This provides those on the street the opportunity to approach cars to ask for money. They move slowly, Styrofoam cups in shaky hands. In six minutes, three women approach my car. My friend's mouth drops open.

Holy shit, these girls look just like us, she says.

---

[3] A line of dialogue from *The Sopranos'* episode "Johnny Cakes" (Season 6)

A shift that may shock those who don't see what I see on a daily basis.

Direct result of the opioid crisis, I guess back.

IV.

I am introduced to my friend's new boyfriend. He asks where I live, and when I tell him, he visibly winces.

I could never live there, he judges. *Even if they are calling it "the next Brooklyn."*

I just laugh and tell him it may not be for everybody.

What I really want to ask him is if he knows his mailman by name, or if his neighbors pull in his garbage cans when he isn't home. I wonder if the people on his block know his parents and grandparents. Do his neighbors spend time shoveling one another's walkways when it snows or help the elderly woman on the block with her groceries? I want to ask him if the bakery in his town calls him personally on Easter or on random Sundays to see if it needs to save special bread for him and his family.

In historic cities like mine, neighborhoods like this still exist, but that never makes the news.

Force of Forgetting

Featuring Taylor Belle

Sunlight creeps in with blackness.
Days of dust and shattered glass
have contorted the face
I once could see
in the frames on my dresser.

At the foot of the mattress,
my broken heart holds mass.
When God and I touch base,
He tells me
you're just settlin' for lesser.

I'll miss you longer
than you ever would've stayed.
That's what writers do,
how we make it through
being betrayed.

These sheets remember you.
The pillows
and the floorboards, too.

These sheets remember you.
The pens
and the ink stains, too.

This is the force of forgetting you.

You disremember with ease,
but you still conquer my thoughts.

I cannot scream anymore
at your tone-deaf heart;
it all hurts too damn much.

I write it down to free
and relieve my stomach knots.
The words pour and pour and pour
out, and I fall apart
as my paper and tears make love.

You'll remain in my words
longer than you did my bed.
You won't ever change,
and so you became
fodder instead.

These sheets remember you.
The pillows
and the floorboards, too.

These sheets remember you.
The pens
and the ink stains, too.

This is the force of forgetting you.
This is the force of forgetting you.

Listen to "Force of Forgetting":
www.thealiciacook.com/taylorbelle

They Knocked Down the Gazebo

Snow smothers most of the noise,
but not the howling of the wind or
the roaring of the ocean.

Everything else is quiet though,
even my mind. For once.

When was the last time I heard the gasp of each breath?

I take it all in because
I don't think I'll be back.

I've outgrown this town.

I can no longer button up the familiar air.
I can no longer slip the beach blocks over my head.
The streetlights and stop signs come up short,
shrunken.

For today though,
I squeeze myself into Third Avenue

one
last
time

because at one point not only was this the only place
that fit, it was the only place I knew, and it's hard to
say goodbye.

No matter what,
it is always hard to say goodbye.

Vellichor & Venom

I am standing in front of the limited self-help section
of a bookstore in the Hamptons.

An associate walks up to me and asks, *Do you know
what you are looking for?*

She seems a bit too curious, too eager; like she has too
often seen seemingly put-together people with full
bank accounts and pretty eyes stroll in from off the
street and expose their demons in front of these same
shelves.

Her delivery is too pointed, as if she were wondering,
*What's wrong with this one? Eating disorder? Daddy
issues? Prescription pill addiction?*

As we stand there, of course I know what I am
looking for in the Goddamn self-help section. Help.
For myself.

I stare blankly for a moment and blink hard twice
before responding, *Do you have anything on what to do
once you fail as a wife, cousin, sister, and human being
in general?*

Her lips part and she mumbles something about a
book like that not being on the shelf. She must be
used to flaws staying beneath one's skin, where many
believe they belong. My honesty does not sit well on
her petite shoulders.

I finish the conversation.

Well, there's a market for it.

With that, the spineless woman leaves me to peruse the book spines on my own, as I intended.

Ready, Set . . .

Start running after yourself.
The person you yearn to become
will never slow down for you,
will never wait for you to

collect
your
courage.

The person you want to leave behind
will do everything in its power to keep you
from catching up to your own potential.

Though that voice cannot be silenced,
it can be passed
and no one hates being outpaced more
than the person you used to be.
The person always
so used to seeing you a

few
paces
behind.

Hope

Featuring Ada Pasternak

Been down and out,
filled with doubt,
had this little heart of mine
kicked around.

All of this hurt
won't break my soft.
What is gone
is never lost.

There's still hope in this hook,
belief in the bridge,
that all of these scars
are proof that I lived.

There's still hope in this hook,
belief that tomorrow
will hold a silver lining
to all of this sorrow.

On the sunniest day,
the sky can seem gray,
but all of my warmth
can't be taken away.

All of these battles,
they've made me fierce.
Know that my faith
cannot be pierced.

There's still hope in this hook,
belief in the bridge,
that all of these scars
are proof that I lived.

There's still hope in this hook,
belief that tomorrow
will hold a silver lining
to all of this sorrow.

'Cause crying doesn't make me weak.
It's my soul, just trying to speak.
Oh, I don't want to go to sleep,
knowing that I could've done better than this.
(Knowing that I could've done better than this.)

There's still hope in this hook,
belief in the bridge,
that all of these scars
are proof that I lived.

There's still hope in this hook,
belief that tomorrow
will hold a silver lining
to all of this sorrow.

'Cause crying doesn't make me weak.
This is my heart just trying to speak.

Listen to "Hope": www.thealiciacook.com/adapasternak

I Lose My Appetite Worrying If You've Eaten

You need to stop internalizing other people's pain, my mother tells me on the phone. *It's not healthy.* She is right; I have done this all of my life. Like an overused sponge, I soak up all the sadness around me, feel it as if it were my own, and expect it not to seep into my own life.

Don't be blinded by your own light, she cautions.
And don't get hurt by pain that doesn't belong to you.

But if I'm not pained by their pain, I have not earned the right to be overjoyed by their joy.

Building Bomb Shelters

We build walls in order to keep people out,
to protect ourselves from pain.

I do not believe these walls are constructed
with bricks and cement
but with ivy and vines and branches
that grow freely around us,
fertilized by the ache.

We lay the foundation for these walls,
we continue to water the hurt.

Stop watering.
Stop spending time with rain clouds.
Instead, wear the sun on your face.

The walls will crumble,
gates and doors and windows
will take shape,
and you will be able
to begin to

let the light in.

Guessing Genetics

His raven hair and my blue eyes.

It is brought to our attention regularly. A dreamy vision paired with pressure. His raven hair and my blue eyes. Surface stuff that paints a pretty, nuclear picture. While they pair his dominant with my recessive genes, all I could think of is his indecisiveness with my selfishness. His neat-freak tendencies with my manic behavior. His soft-spoken nature with my short temper. His first-responder training and my habit of never wearing my seat belt. His light with my dark. My light with his dark. I find myself thanking God that my genes are the recessive ones because he possesses more good in his pinky finger than I do in my whole body.

But yes,
his raven hair
with my blue eyes
would be beautiful.

Written October 2, 2017 (TW)

I woke up to the profound sound
of a world smothered silent.
The sun shone through the curtains.
It would have been a beautiful day,
I'm certain,
if it weren't colored by violence.

People running for their lives.
I don't shield my eyes.
I'm so desensitized
and I'm mad at myself for that.

I've been watching wars
on my TV screen
ever since I was fifteen
and I'm mad at the world for that.

A shadow cast,
flags at half-mast,
knowing this won't be the last
time I'll be afraid.

They say love makes
the world go 'round,
but the ones with love in their hearts
are the ones gunned down.

What do we gain from all of this pain?
Most just post prayers online.
It's hard to feel safe at all

when someone gets twenty-one guns
down a hall
with plans to traumatize.

The Earth can't keep us safe;
it's not its role, not its place
to lead us to better days.
Only we can guide each other.

Too many innocents slain.
A date forever bloodstained.
Our faith in humanity strains.
Only we can save each other.

Collective sighs.
No reason why
all these people have to die
from a horror so stark.

They say light shall
conquer the dark,
but every time terror strikes,
we lose a bit of our spark.

We must trust
there are less of them
and more of us
in this world.

Bombilating Brains at Breakfast

Can you please speak up? I am having trouble
hearing you. The flies on the walls of my mind are
contributing their two cents again, rather loudly.

> *Buzzzzz – I'd like to see you turn*
> *this mess into poetry – buzzzzz.*

I shake my head and my thoughts fall back into place
and I am able to focus on you once more. I quickly
catch up to the conversation you think we are having.

My mother says I did the same thing in school.
Teachers complained to her regularly that I zoned out
in class; but when they tried to catch me lost in the
lesson, I'd come back to reality and somehow manage
to answer their questions correctly.

You let it slide. You let all my moods slide. You are
confusing my neurosis for artistic depth again.

You've learned the deeper you fall into me, the
stickier I become, and the harder I am to leave. You
will think you caught me, but you are the one who is
stuck; I was never really here to begin with.

Twenty2

Each day as I am rushing through my life, the key to my parents' house jingles on my keychain. The chiseled metal opens a portal to home. To my yesterdays. To my family.

To the familiar.

Each day I touch this key, see this key, and think to myself, *I should really visit home.* Yet, I cannot remember for the life of me the last time this key turned in its lock. I cannot recall the last time I saw the sign in the entryway.

We'll leave the light on for you.

I feel myself taking all that is 69.8 miles away for granted.

I should really visit home,
life has been so hectic though,
maybe next week.

Sonder

I am fourth in line today at the doughnut and coffee shop on Bloomfield Avenue. The two guys at the register see there are more Jets doughnuts remaining than Giants. They surmise there must be more Giants fans in the area because of this, and I think their logic is sound.

The other guy in front of me is wearing black socks with sandals and has his hair slicked back. His attire and demeanor lead me to assume he works at the BMW dealership across the street.

Assumptions. That's all we make.

We never really know the strangers around us, but that doesn't stop us from assuming something about them one way or another. I think it's more human curiosity than jumping to conclusions or judging.

The man with the slicked-back hair gets his coffee and I watch him walk back across the street to the dealership. I peek over my shoulder and wonder for a moment what the person behind me is assuming about me, but I shake it off. It does not matter.

Limelight Breakup

I am really pissed
I pay a therapist
for all this shit.

That brown hair tie
is definitely not mine,
you claim otherwise.

Now I'm crying
because you're lying
about your cell dying.

You always hated
that I was makin'
somethin' of myself.

Jealous and frustrated
I was celebrated,
so you'd fuck someone else.

You found it all too stressful,
my being successful,
and grew resentful.

Were totally opposed
to me working toward goals
so you'd poke holes

in my self-esteem,
you'd plot and scheme,
break me with your deceit.

You were never okay
with the way
I was growing up.

You would slip away
and then you'd complain,
say I didn't care enough.

Never met a man
so narcissistic,
so chauvinistic.
I was your fan,
but you,
you were my critic.

And now,
we're finished.

Save—Don't Save—Cancel

All the things I've wanted to tell you since you left are lodged inside my throat and in half-dialed numbers and e-mail drafts. Like how it'd be easier to move on if the only marks you left on my life were scars; but the beautiful imprint you left on my heart will remain long after your pillow regains its shape.

I want you to know that even foreign elevators and hotel lobbies smell like you, but your ghost doesn't live here anymore. And just the other day, I saw my shadow for the first time in what feels like a lifetime. It was as if it appeared just to convince me that though I may feel one-dimensional right now,

I am still flesh and bone and here.

And with each day that passes, I become more strong, more fierce. And with each day that passes, my heart forgets you a little bit more.

Loose Threads Get Lost

I sit at my desk and notice a thread has come loose in the hem of my dress. All I do is pull it once, with not much effort, and the thread is separated from the fabric.

At first, to the naked eye, it does not seem as though the rest of the dress has been affected, but the material knows and begins to fall apart between each wear and wash, slowly at first, then all at once.

I can't help but wonder if the dress would have survived had that one thread not come loose. Thread is not made of steel or wood but a material one can bite through with ease, split between just two fingers. Is a thread, so hairline thin, so fragile, capable of separating an entire entity?

Yes.

I like to think families are stitched together by invisible threads. Some whose lengths extend down familiar hallways, others that span across miles and continents; but they are sewn together nonetheless, connected through blood and tears and laughter and birthdays.

Life has a tendency to pick at these threads—for better or for worse. Things happen and they are tightened, brought closer together; things happen and they are torn apart, ripped at the seams. Just like my dress, a family's stitching can be altered.

Some things destroy a family's fabric more than others. A family's undoing is not a beautiful disentanglement, but an ugly severance.

I can't help but wonder if the family would have survived had that one thread not come loose.

My Fifth Sense

When you and I met,
you smelled of summer
at the Jersey Shore and
I wanted to bottle up the
entire four seconds.

I felt my world shift.
I felt my heart expand
and change and make room.
It was the first time
I was acutely aware that
what was playing out in front of me
would permanently change my life.

I felt it all—
my pounding heart,
your piercing eyes;
my nervousness added
to the stickiness of the humidity in the air.

I was woken up that day.
It was as if I had slept through
the other three seasons
and had just opened my eyes
in the dead heat of July.

Everyone Else, Then Me

Our lives are just going in different directions,
        you said, with little inflection.

We are just in different places right now,
        you added, then walked out.

Honey, there will be others,
        promised my mother.

When it comes to true love, you'll just know it,
        wrote a cliché-riddled poet.

You can do so much better,
        scribbled a friend, in a letter.

You are stronger than you think,
        diagnosed my shrink.

Ten years is nothing, you're still so young,
        a math equation, from someone.

I know someone who would be perfect for you,
        another friend said, from her point of view.

I will cry myself dry.
        I will survive.
                I will thrive,
                        said my voice,
                        from deep inside.

Ortley Beach

My toes have danced in many oceans.
My arms and legs have waded in many waters.
My mind has imagined reaching their horizons.

Still, nothing compares to my ocean,
whose tides I have known my whole life.
Whose winter temperatures never kept me away.
Whose whitecaps wrapped around my skin.
Whose sprays cleansed, never stung.
Whose seas healed my cuts and broken hearts.
Whose waves I swam in with my father.
Whose sand collected in my bathing suits
and in my family's drains.
Whose waters watched me grow.
Whose salt helped shape my molecules
and played a distinct role in who I became.

This small piece of a vast ocean
raised me—her changing tides
assured me that even at my lowest,
I, too, would rise again.

Just trust time, she would sing.
The moon will reset us both.

Marie

I can't remember how you used to say my name.
Which sounds ridiculous because I still remember my
name, of course, and the sound of your voice; but I
can't close my eyes and hear you say those three
syllables anymore.

The tone, the inflection, the warmth.

Even more strange, I do clearly remember the way
you used to utter those nicknames you gave me; like
when you would call me by my middle name. But not
my name, and the harder I try to conjure it, the more
distant your echo becomes.

It's barely a whisper now. White noise.

Maybe that is a good thing. Maybe another saying my
name over and over ever since I fell in love again has
finally drowned you out of my psyche.

Barnegat Bay

Even though I sit here with my solitude, I am not lonely. When you have good memories stowed away, you're never really alone.

A lifetime of reminiscences keep me company today as the rain plays its music on water's surface. I am perched at the front of the dock, my feet float freely off the ledge of the pier. My father used to take me here to catch crabs with drop lines. The water laps against the post, even spraying me from time to time. I lick the salt from my lips. I breathe in the smell of the bay at dusk. The smell would cause some to scowl, to pinch their noses. I suppose the smell could be repulsive, if it weren't tied into my bloodstream and genesis.

Palermo

The tour guide keeps mentioning the blending of *the old and the new* in the city. *The old,* beautiful ivy balconies, five-ton chandeliers, and streets of marble. *The new,* graffiti attacking their government and police, litter in the streets.

Stray dogs run rampant but don't really run. They just lie there because they are too weak. We buy a loaf of bread out of the trunk of a man's car for one euro and spend the rest of the afternoon ripping pieces from it and tossing it to the animals.

A homeless man gets a hold of a piece
and shares it with a dog.

The best may already be behind us,
but humanity is still here.

I'll Take It (A Duet)

Featuring Codey Bearden & Arrie Bozeman

I met a tall boy who played the drums,
I never even learned his last name.
But his tongue lit me like a flame,
and that's enough to call it love.

I saw you walk into the room,
not the same ol' twist of fate.
If there's a Heaven, well I found the gate,
and that's enough to call it love.

He jumped from city to city,
I just knew we wouldn't make it.
He said my eyes were pretty,
if there's a chance of love, I'll take it

We didn't have to last forever,
to be makin' this beautiful music together.

Here we are on the front porch swingin'
I play the music, you do the singin'.
I don't know how this story goes,
but if you give me this dance,
I'll take it.

He liked my voice and the rips in my jeans,
told him I liked to sing my own songs
mostly about where I've gone wrong,
and he called me the girl of his dreams.

You came back to the show the next week.
I saw you singin' along.
Knew every word to every song,
I can't tell if I'm awake.

She wore all those fancy clothes.
Miss Corporate in some big buildin'.
She didn't mind my flip-flop toes,
the future's in her eye, God willin'.

We didn't have to last forever,
to be makin' this beautiful music together.

Here we are on the front porch swingin'
I play the music, you do the singin'.
I don't know how this story goes,
but if you give me your hand,
I'll take it.

Still, you come to see me play.
        A couple years gone by,
it's our ten-year anniversary,
        and you still blow my mind.

We didn't have to last forever,
to be making this beautiful music together.

Here we are on the front porch swingin'
I play the music, you do the singin'.
I don't know how this story goes,
but if you give me your heart,
I'll take it.

This could go on forever,
makin' this beautiful music together.

Listen to "I'll Take It (A Duet)":
www.thealiciacook.com/codeybearden

Apple Skin Stuck Between Teeth

Before tonight, the last time I baked an apple crisp, it was for you and I forgot to peel the apples so they went in, skin and all. You ate it anyway even though you and I both knew it wasn't my best. In hindsight, spitting out apple flesh together on the couch that night seems fitting because you weren't the best version of yourself when you ate it and I wasn't the best version of myself when I made it and we weren't the best version of us when we were sitting there, legs crossed, together. So now, as I slide my latest apple crisp out of my new oven in my new home, I can tell by the smell of the warmth that this one is the best I've ever made—which seems fitting because I am finally the best version of myself, too.

More Cherry Blossoms Than D.C.

Where winter slammed into my body, leaving bruises
and soreness behind, spring made love to me. Melted,
slowly, into my marrow.

You place a cherry blossom behind my ear and say it
matches my dress and lips.

We take refuge from reality under the pink trees
in Branch Brook Park that will only stay as beautiful
as this for another two days.

The wind dances with the branches and the petals
rain down, and we pretend they are velvet raindrops
falling from the sky.

There's magic to be found in days that begin quite
ordinarily if you just open yourself up to possibilities.

EWR -> BCN

We are having dinner together at the airport before our flight.

I can't gaze lovingly into your eyes, even if I wanted to, because obstructing our views of each other are two tablets.

Please place your orders through these tablets. You can also play games on them while you wait for your meal. But you can't play against one another; the tablets are not synced together. They don't communicate, explains the server.

We are all so disconnected, I respond.

We order a $42 bottle of red wine that retails at $9 and entrees through the device, not the person I am supposed to be tipping at 20 percent.

We are all so disconnected.

As we eat, a blaring alarm goes off throughout the airport and continues to scream throughout the whole meal.

We're not in 2001 anymore, Toto.

Sixteen years ago, this would have caused mass panic and hysteria, but in 2017, not one person flinches.

We are all so disconnected.

Counting Sirens

I have my cheap headphones in my ears, so I hear the boat's motor and the late-summer wind over my music. The sky matches the water today. It is hard to tell where the horizon line sleeps.

If somber had a color, it would be gray.

I appreciate the irony when I see the *no wake zone* signs bobbing violently as we approach the Thomas J. Mathis Bridge. Cars roar above us like extinct creatures.

It is the type of hazy day where my mother would warn us about applying sunscreen. Clouds momentarily break and the water sparkles. We used to say mermaids swam beneath wherever the water glistened.

I count the sun glitter patches to myself until I lose count.

Five thousand mermaids, I estimate, *are swimming alongside my heart today.*

Told Myself

Featuring Carly Moffa

I dreamt of you in a reclusive way,
imagined us to be timeless.
But you were never really here,
your eyes were always off chasing dragons.

You responded in an elusive way,
nonchalant and indecisive.
On our one-way trip to nowhere,
I pretended to not hear your silence.

"I wish I never met you,"
a phrase I could never get through.

Told myself
even if our ending couldn't change,
I would still do everything the same,
because touching you for that long
was better than never touching you at all.

Built us up in a delusive way,
stargazing from the cold basement.
We forgive those with serpent spines,
it's the fault line of our generation.

You led me on in an abusive way,
played my idiosyncrasies.
My love of weaving lies in rhymes,
my torrid affair with hyperbole.

"I wish I could forget you,"
a lie designed to upset you.

Told myself
if I saw true colors through gray,
I would grab my heart and run away,
because loving you for that long
doesn't count if it was never love at all.

Then, I forgot you in a human way,
became strong when it mattered most.
My heart, it became my weapon,
drew a line in the sand, planned my revolt.

Then, you mourned me in a consuming way,
crushed you with the weight of my ghost.
You finally learned your lesson
when ash from last words got caught in your throat.

"I changed, come back, I beg you,"
a plea meant to make me swoon.

Told myself
I'd never again dream of your face,
but I haunt you all over the place.
I needed you here for so long,
and now I do not need you here at all.

Listen to "Told Myself": www.thealiciacook.com/
carlymoffa

An Untrained Eye Will Miss Everything

Life is split into *before* and *after*. We capture the *befores* while they are *nows* in photographs.

I keep a photo tucked into my dresser mirror. On the surface, there is nothing remarkable about this photo of me and two people I love smiling under my mother's favorite tree in the backyard.

By the budding blossoms, I will always remember this photo was taken in early spring. On the precipice of not having to wear tights beneath dresses.

There is nothing remarkable about this photo of me and two people I love smiling under my mother's favorite tree in the backyard. By the easy smiles on our faces, I can tell this was the last early spring before everything changed. That was the last photo taken before everything changed.

There is nothing remarkable about this photo of me and two people I love smiling under my mother's favorite tree in the backyard. The photo is not centered or as focused as some of the photos we have taken since that day.

Not all the changes since have been bad. However, we no longer smile that effortlessly anymore. I let this photo of me and two people I love smiling under my mother's favorite tree in the backyard greet me each morning because someone told me once we live life forwards but remember it backwards and that was one backwards day where I remember everything was actually fine. I like to remember we existed like that once. Actually fine. It gives me hope that we can one day be that way again. Actually fine.

70 in December

Featuring Christina Hart (@christinakaylenhart)

I cannot keep up with the traffic
in the left lane of the Turnpike today.
Maybe the sappy song on the radio
is slowing down my pace.

Whatever the reason,
I keep having to get over one lane
to allow for the faster cars to zip by.

We are nearing the holidays and
it's seventy degrees and sunny.
Why is everyone in such a rush?
I want to take my time with today,
especially since the forecast is
calling for winter tomorrow.

They say our hearts will
thaw out sometime
near spring and
the weather is just another
thing for us to avoid.

I cannot keep up with the
sweeping up of all the
things we should be saying.

It is too warm today
and tomorrow will be too cold
and the next day will come too soon
and will we ever really be satisfied with right now?

You Are Not the Sun

The pictures no longer cause my stomach to drop into my feet. I no longer search for your fingerprints on things around the house just to remind myself that we shared time and space. I no longer experience what could only be explained as *the heartbreak sweats*; the elevated breathing, the nausea.

I do not love you anymore.
I do not miss you anymore.
I am not angry with you anymore.

But, most importantly.

I am no longer angry with myself for shrinking my size and talent just so you could feel tall. I am no longer angry with myself for downplaying my aspirations and accomplishments just so you could take center stage.

I spent so much time trying to be less.
Less driven.
Less acknowledged.
Less than you.

I couldn't be contained.

I no longer live in a world
that revolves around your ego.
You are not a life source.
You are not the sun.

It's the best feeling in the world to know
I haven't just moved on,
I've eclipsed you.

A Clandestine Operation

We dress in plain clothes. We order coffee at the same café you frequent. We pick up the dry cleaning and go food shopping. We get up every morning and start our day. Just like you, we forget our umbrellas when we need them most. We fold towels and put socks away. We are unassuming and welcome flying under the radar. There are a lot of us out there. You might have to ask ten questions before you discover what rages beneath our surfaces. You'd never know what we've done simply by looking at our faces, but we can identify one another with ease.

We are survivors.

We survived even when the ones we loved did not. We survived even when we thought we couldn't last another day, another minute, another second. We survived even when those closest to us believed we wouldn't . . . couldn't.

We faced the worst and beat the odds.
We faced the worst and didn't become a statistic.
We faced the worst and lived to tell our tales.

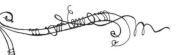

Footprints

Featuring Codey Bearden

I've never been the smartest
one in any room,
but I know if I work hard, I've
seen what I can do.
It's the same old block I've walked
at least a time or two,
and it keeps going.

I'm just trying to let you know:

I don't want to be famous,
that's not to say the stars
aren't where I'm aimin'.
Walkin' 'round this world with
no shoes but a lot of soul,
just trying to leave a
little footprint when I go.

There's been times I thought for sure
that I was done,
fell flat on my face before
I had begun.
Not every swing I take
will be a home run,
but I'll keep swinging.

Seen dreams wash down the gutter
in front of my eyes.
Spent time on my knees prayin'
for stars to align.

I've run for days to end back
at the starting line,
but I keep runnin'.

They pushed me down, then said I fell.
I got back up without their help.
Threw all I had in a wishing well.
Want to leave my mark, raise some hell.
I'm striving for greatness, but

I don't want to be famous,
that's not to say the stars
aren't where I'm aimin'.
Walkin' 'round this world with
no shoes but a lot of soul,
just trying to leave a
little footprint when I go.

Listen to "Footprints":
www.thealiciacook.com/codeybearden

I Hope My Voice Doesn't Skip

When there is nothing left to say,

you   stop.

You   take in a breath.
You   let out a breath.
You   listen.

Do not stutter through made-up words for the sake of hearing your own voice.

When there is nothing left to say,

you   leave.

Do not stumble through made-up words for the sake of holding on.

When there is nothing left to say,

you   let go.

You do not allow your heart to suffer.
It has been too good to you to allow it to suffer.

The
End

Liner Notes

This book began like all my other work: scattered. Jotted down on napkins and in various notebooks and e-mail drafts, recorded in voice memos. It came together thanks to so many amazing people I am fortunate enough to call my family, friends, and colleagues.

First, my parents. Growing up, I never realized how rare it was to have parents who had my back and who supported my artistic ventures until I landed in the creative world and learned many parents didn't believe their kids could "make it" as creatives. You guys never wavered, your faith in me never lessened. You never suggested I study anything other than literature and journalism. I want to thank you for that because if you tried to steer me in another direction when I was younger, I may not have the life I have today, and that would be terribly sad, because I love my life.

Mom, in a world of "yes men" you are my guidepost. Your honesty on all of this work was blunt and necessary. I'll never forget in November 2016 when you told me to throw the whole manuscript out and start over. You told me not to "force it," to take my time, and to just live my life. I took your advice, and I am happy I did. I am so proud of this body of work. You are my first and most trusted editor.

Dad, I want to thank you for playing your records, (yes, even the times you blasted Pavarotti over the intercoms at 6 a.m.). Thank you for exposing me to all different artists and styles, from the crooners to disco to classic rock to doo-wop. People laugh when I tell them the first CD I ever bought with my "own money" was Tony Bennett's *Perfectly Frank*, but I am so glad! You instilled in me the importance of knowing the artist and not just memorizing the lyrics. I remember when you would quiz me, "Who sang this?" "Who wrote that?" "What was Sinatra's nickname?" "What movie did 'Steppin' Out With My Baby' appear in?" This trivia made me curious to learn more about the life of the artist—the story behind the song.

To the rest of my family, especially my sister, Kellie, I want to thank you all for just "getting" it. For understanding, from all the way back when we were kids filming movies I directed in our basement, that I was going to create for a living, which would mean writing about our lives.

To my Michael and his fam-jam (except you, Ant, because you are *the worst*), I feel your excitement daily, and it means the world to me that you have embraced this crazy journey. Thank you for rooting for me. I love you all (except Ant).

To Jess Cook—my cousin in Heaven—this is all actually happening. Can you believe it?!

To my ever-so-patient friends who have yet to shun me for lapsing on returning phone calls and/or texts—I love you.

To my girl, J.R. Rogue, who appears in this book, I will say this 'til the day I die: You are the best writer to ever do this thing. Oh, and to you and Ms. Kat Savage—thank you for creating such amazing writing prompts. The results of a few ended up in this book.

To the musicians who donated their time and talent to this vision: Ada Pasternak, Highland Kites, Codey Bearden and Arrie Bozeman, Taylor Belle, Caitlin Mahoney, Christopher Andrews, Carly Moffa, Kristin Michelle Elizabeth, and Renee Mazza. This book wouldn't be what it is without each of you. I am forever indebted you returned my messages. I hope we keep creating together. You deserve ALL the streams and Grammys.

To Jordan Emanuel for connecting me with the ever-so-talented Caitlin Mahoney. There's nothing better than women supporting women.

To Christina Hart, the first writer to read this collection and provide the feedback only another writer could provide: THANK. GOD. FOR. YOU. I am so happy we had a chance to write together on this one. Next round of ridiculously portioned nachos is on me.

To Adam Castro *mostly* for coming up with the titles "Hypnic Jerk" and "Traffic, Signs." You are great. RANKED.

To the Andrews McMeel Publishing team, especially Patty, for taking a chance on me back in 2016 and again in 2018; and to my agent, Byrd, for emailing me two years ago and for having an even cooler name. Let's keep doing this. It's fun.

Lastly, to the READERS. What did I do right to deserve all of you? You're all so awesome and passionate. I love keeping up with all of you on social media and chatting about music and Buffy and everything else. I hope this book resonates with you as much as *Stuff I've Been Feeling Lately* did. This one, honestly, is even closer to my heart. Even more personal. I hope it helps you feel less alone and more understood. I wouldn't be living out this dream if it weren't for every single one of you. I am so excited to finally get this collection in your hands, and hopefully in your hearts as well! Stick with me. I won't let you down.

About the Author

Alicia Cook is an established writer and award-winning activist living in New Jersey whose work has been seen on HuffPost, USA Today, Bustle, and CNN, to name a few.

Named one of the best "Instagram poets" by *Teen Vogue,* her poetry is usually unfixed and covers various topics and emotions, most notably grief. Her bestselling book of poetry, *Stuff I've Been Feeling Lately,* was a finalist in the 2016 Goodreads Choice Awards.

Cook, the 2017 recipient of the "Special Voices" award in Trenton, advocates to break the stigma surrounding families affected by drug addiction. Her essay series, *The Other Side of Addiction,* written in honor of her cousin Jessica Cook, has developed a worldwide readership. Her efforts were featured on the episode "A Family Disease" by the Emmy-nominated documentary series *Here's the Story.* The episode has gone on to be nominated in several film festivals.

Cook is currently the Director of Institutional Communications and Campaign Marketing at Bloomfield College. In 2017, *On the Green,* the magazine she writes for the College, won the platinum award in the MarCom Awards, the organization's highest honor.

Cook earned a bachelor's degree (2008) in English Literature with a concentration in Journalism and a master's degree in Business Administration with a concentration in Risk Management (2012).

Also by Alicia Cook:

Stuff I've Been Feeling Lately

Heroin is the Worst Thing to Ever Happen to Me

Follow Alicia:

@thealiciacook

@the_alicia_cook

www.thealiciacook.com

#ihopemyvoicedoesntskip

Andrews McMeel Publishing
a division of Andrews McMeel Universal
1130 Walnut Street, Kansas City, Missouri 64106

www.andrewsmcmeel.com

18 19 20 21 22 BVG 10 9 8 7 6 5 4 3 2 1

ISBN: 978-1-4494-9424-7

Library of Congress Control Number: 2017962449

iStock.com/Emilia_Szymanek

Editor: Patty Rice
Art Director: Julie Barnes
Production Editor: Elizabeth A. Garcia
Production Manager: Cliff Koehler

ATTENTION: SCHOOLS AND BUSINESSES
Andrews McMeel books are available at quantity discounts
with bulk purchase for educational, business, or sales
promotional use. For information, please e-mail the
Andrews McMeel Publishing Special Sales Department:
specialsales@amuniversal.com.